Joan C. Webb

EVERYDAY
Wisdom

Spiritual Refreshment
for Women

BARBOUR
PUBLISHING

Writing and compilation by Joan C. Webb in association with Snapdragon Group℠ Tulsa, Oklahoma, USA.

ISBN 978-1-60260-776-7

Member of the
Evangelical Christian
Publishers Association

Printed in India.

Contents

My [daughter], if you accept
my words and store up
my commands within you,
turning your ear to wisdom
and applying your heart to
understanding, and if you call
out for insight and cry aloud for
understanding, and if you look
for it as for silver and search for
it as for hidden treasure, then you
will understand the fear of the LORD
and find the knowledge of God.
For the LORD gives wisdom,
and from his mouth come
knowledge and understanding.

PROVERBS 2:1–6 NIV

Introduction

What a remarkable opportunity you have!
Imagine becoming a wise, knowledgeable,
and discerning woman—whether you have
one, two, or zero degrees. Regardless of your
age, position, or season, you're invited to
walk with and learn from the source of all
wisdom, God Himself. He knows you better
than you know yourself, and He cares—about
your secret dreams, financial struggles,
career woes, and family dynamics.

Everyday Wisdom was created to help you develop a richer relationship with our awesome God and give you a glimpse of His knowledge on the life topics that concern you. Our prayer is that while reading these words, you'll grow to recognize your options, make wise daily choices, and take intentional action. That's what God wants for you. Now isn't that amazing?

Acceptance

Don't jump to conclusions—
there may be a perfectly good
explanation for what you just saw.

PROVERBS 25:8 MSG

You cry at movies; your sister doesn't. Your spouse shares openly with anyone he meets; you prefer to take time getting to know someone first. You enjoy working alone; your boss works best on a team. Your mother gives instant solutions; you like mulling over the options. It's easy to jump to conclusions when another person doesn't think or act as you do. But when you suspend judgment of the differing ideas and opinions of others, you're a wise—and gracious—woman.

> To get wisdom is to
> love oneself; to keep
> understanding is to prosper.

PROVERBS 19:8 NRSV

If you can accept yourself, you will probably be able to more readily accept the idiosyncrasies of others. If you are patient with yourself, you will almost certainly be more tolerant toward your loved ones. If you have learned to forgive yourself, you're likely to find you can more easily forgive someone else. Self-respect increases as you stay committed to gaining a heart of wisdom. This attitude splashes onto your other relationships, and acceptance gradually becomes a way of life.

Aging

Aging isn't for wimps! It's true. Whether
you're twenty-five or seventy-five, there are
probably things about getting older that you
don't appreciate. Extra pounds. Hormone
imbalances. Another gray hair. Yet, as a
God-honoring woman, you probably have
one thing that only grows more beautiful
and amazing with age—a heart of wisdom.
The longer you live and the more wisdom
you accumulate, the brighter your influence.
So congratulate yourself. You're not a wimp,
you're a star.

The glory of the young is their strength; the gray hair of experience is the splendor of the old.

PROVERBS 20:29 NLT

The expression "Generation Gap" became popular in the 1960s, although it probably existed in some uncoined sense throughout history. Young people don't get their grandparents, and the over-fifty crowd can't figure out their juniors. Some sense a standoff. But the truth is, there is beauty on both sides of the gap. Young people possess stamina and a lust for life, while those who've been around awhile are reservoirs of experience and wisdom. In God, we are glorious at any age.

Appearances

Humans are satisfied
with whatever looks good;
God probes for what is good.

PROVERBS 16:2 MSG

Like many women, you probably enjoy looking nice when you go out for a special occasion. You want a hairstyle that flatters your face, clothes that fit well, and a little makeup to enhance your eyes and cheeks. God likes it when you feel good about your appearance. Still though, He cares more about the inner you. He wants to cultivate what's good about you socially, emotionally, mentally, and spiritually. Join with Him in cultivating the beauty that's inside you.

> We justify our
> actions by appearances;
> God examines our motives.
>
> PROVERBS 21:2 MSG

People—women and men—want to look good to others. Sometimes we do this by name-dropping, pretending we don't need help, or reciting our credentials and achievements. At other times we do it by being overly nice, overworking, and rarely saying no. Both approaches to trying to keep our appearances up can wear us out. Relief comes when you admit your need, allow God to purify your motives, and then just enjoy honoring Him as the person He created you to be.

Assurance

The LORD directs our steps,
so why try to understand
everything along the way?

PROVERBS 20:24 NLT

Are you tired of trying so hard to make sure
you do everything just right? Do you long
to hear God whispering that He's with you
and in control? Then you're like many other
busy and overworked women. God knows
your desire to love others, serve, and make
wise choices. He hears your genuine prayer
for help and strength. And He's answering.
So lean back and take a deep breath. You are
loved more than you'll ever know.

The Lord will be your confidence
and will keep your foot
from being caught.

PROVERBS 3:26 NRSV

Life is risky. With these risks come adventure, fulfillment—and uncertainty. Are you starting a career and overwhelmed with all you must learn? Are you a new mother, wondering how you'll raise this tiny person who awakens you in the night? Although you enjoy your independence, do you wonder whether you'll ever find a mate? Are you facing big decisions now that your husband is gone? Whatever your challenge, give your doubt to God. He'll never leave you. Never.

Authenticity

The Lord looks deep
inside people and searches
through their thoughts.

PROVERBS 20:27 NCV

If you're like most women who've
participated in relationship surveys, you
want someone to hear your heart and not
be frightened off. Although you've been
disappointed in relationships before, you
still desire to be loved for who you really are.
Good news! God is not surprised by what you
feel, say, or think. He knows you inside and
out and loves you just the way you are. So
drop your guard and be authentic with Him.
He isn't going anywhere.

People's thoughts can be
like a deep well, but someone
with understanding can find
the wisdom there.

PROVERBS 20:5 NCV

People have their own answers—or can at
least find them. This is a basic tenet of the
highly successful industry of life coaching.
Life coaches ask powerful questions that
help their clients discover those hidden
answers, move past their status quo, and
grow. You have your own answers, too.
They may be lodged deep within you, but
with some authentic sharing and a wise
companion's thoughtful probing, you can
find the wisdom. Ask God to direct you to
this kind of authenticity.

Balance

Do you like honey?
Don't eat too much,
or it will make you sick!

PROVERBS 25:16 NLT

All work and no play makes Jack a dull boy." (By the way, all work and no play can make Jill a dull girl as well!) You've probably heard this age-old axiom countless times. Yet the opposite is also true. All play and no work makes Jack and Jill uninteresting, not to mention unproductive. Focusing on one area of life to the detriment of its counterpoint is not wise. You can discover balance and thrive.

She gets up before dawn to prepare
breakfast for her household and plan
the day's work for her servant girls.

PROVERBS 31:15 NLT

You've got a lot to do. Each of your roles
shouts for attention. How can you do it all?
You can't. You're only one woman, although
a caring, capable one. As a new employee,
first-time mother, or start-up business
owner, you encounter huge learning curves.
You'll need to make adjustments. You may
need to wake up early or ask for specialized
help. This phase won't last forever. Give
yourself a break. Do what you need to do to
maintain balance.

Beauty

"She'll garland your life
with grace, she'll festoon
your days with beauty."

PROVERBS 4:9 MSG

You are a beautiful creation of God. As
a woman with a heart for God, you seek
wisdom and understanding, and it shows.
Grace reflects in your eyes as you speak with
kindness and encouragement. Magazine
advertisements and Hollywood may tell
you that to be one of the "beautiful people"
you must maintain an ideal weight, banish
wrinkles, schedule regular pedicures,
highlight your hair—and more. While
all these regimens are fine, wisdom's
loveliness in you far exceeds them all.

Charm is deceitful and
beauty is passing, but a
woman who fears the LORD,
she shall be praised.

PROVERBS 31:30 NKJV

Do you ever feel society's pressure to
look younger than your years? Dress in
the season's latest fashions? Be your
neighborhood's most charming hostess?
Perhaps you sense this pressure and so
you keep trying. Or maybe you've given up.
Surely you've noticed that birthdays are
inevitable, outer beauty can fade, and charm
can fool. But be encouraged today. As you
continue to honor, respect, and love God,
you become a praiseworthy woman. Are you
smiling yet?

Blessing

The blessing of the LORD
makes one rich.

PROVERBS 10:22 NKJV

God blesses His children. No doubt about it. Just look around you. Your life is richer because of His protection, provision, presence, grace, and love. How can you respond to God's blessing? Gratefully accept Him and all that He gives you. And then bless Him back. Perhaps that seems like the ultimate audacity. The perfect Blesser receiving blessings from His own creation? Yet out of your rich inner resources of blessing, you can honor, revere, and bless the Giver.

By the blessing of the upright
a city is exalted.

PROVERBS 11:11 NRSV

You may not know it, but you have the power to make a significant difference in your neighborhood, city, state, and—consequently—the world. What you believe about life; how you express those beliefs; how you treat your neighbors, acquaintances, governmental leaders, and coworkers reaches further than you may realize. When you bless those around you with your God-given wisdom, you are building up yourself, those around you, and gradually the world you live in.

Boundaries

"I, Wisdom, live together
with good judgment. . . .
I was there when he set the limits
of the seas, so they would not
spread beyond their boundaries."

PROVERBS 8:12, 29 NLT

Wisdom originates with God. When God
designed the world, wisdom watched with
joy as He drew distinct boundaries around
the oceans and seas to protect His other
creation from drowning. It's a picture of the
boundaries He designed for you. You are
not your mother. You are not your friend.
You are not your spouse. No one has a right
to step over your boundary line and take
advantage of you. You are distinct. God
made you that way.

> When you find a friend,
> don't outwear your welcome;
> show up at all hours and
> he'll soon get fed up.

PROVERBS 25:17 MSG

We all want to be loved and accepted. Yet some of us try too hard to make and keep friends. We may work harder than necessary to hold on to a boyfriend. We disregard boundaries, becoming overly enmeshed in another's life to the detriment of our own development. But there's good news. By placing your dependence on God first, you can change. Although transformation won't happen overnight, God will help you respond wisely to the people in your life. Just ask Him.

Business

[God] loves it when
business is aboveboard.

PROVERBS 11:1 MSG

Whether you're a stay-at-home mother, empty nester, CEO, student, teacher, or attorney, God expects you to be honest in all your transactions—at the grocery store, the local bank, with your children and husband, in the boardroom, in court, on your tax forms, and when interacting with your repairman. Maybe you had trustworthy role models when you were growing up; perhaps you didn't. But as an aspiring wise woman, you can keep your everyday business dealings honorable. God will help.

A prudent person foresees danger
and takes precautions.

PROVERBS 22:3 NLT

Wisdom means planning for the worst, anticipating the best, and trusting God with every outcome. Whether you're researching colleges to attend, purchasing a home, getting married, starting a new company, taking care of your aging parents, or have just learned you're pregnant, you'll want to ask intelligent questions and plan for your next steps. God encourages you to think ahead. Seek the advice of trusted friends and associates, take necessary precautions, and then turn the results over to Him.

Busyness

The diligent find freedom
in their work.

PROVERBS 12:24 MSG

It's fun watching a juggler. He tosses and balances balls, knives, hats, and sometimes flaming torches. It appears easy. Yet if you asked, you'd probably discover how many focused and diligent hours he practices. Learning to work without the constant buzz of busyness is like learning a juggling act. Although you want to stop rushing, it feels so impossible that you're tempted to cease trying. But be encouraged. You'll find success if you stay committed to practicing a balanced schedule.

> One who moves too
> hurriedly misses the way.
>
> PROVERBS 19:2 NRSV

Hurry. Faster. Accomplish more. Learn this. Study that. Time's wasting. Do more for God. Messages like these fly around us daily—whether they're blatant or inferred. Perhaps you've sensed the rush and have become too busy, trying to do it all. Now you're tired. How can you change? First, know that God isn't the one pressing the HURRY button. He doesn't want you to dash through life and lose your way. He wants you to slow down and enjoy every minute.

Calmness

Foolish people lose their tempers,
but wise people control theirs.

PROVERBS 29:11 NCV

Feeling angry doesn't automatically mean
you've sinned. Anger is a normal response
to injustice and wrong. God becomes angry
over the disobedience of the people He
loves. Jesus responded angrily to the corrupt
money changers in the temple, but He
didn't sin. It's when anger is allowed to rage
or fester as resentment that it wrecks havoc
with your soul and relationships. You're
wise when you face your anger responsibly,
discover its roots, and partner with God to
control it.

A wise person stays calm
when insulted.

PROVERBS 12:16 NLT

It's difficult to remain calm when criticized, whether the criticism is legitimate or not. On occasion someone may unjustly criticize you merely for the thrill of creating chaos or starting a quarrel. It's not a wise way for them to interact, but it's not your problem. It's theirs. You don't have to fix them or engage in an argument. You can tell them calmly and firmly that you won't tolerate their disrespect. Then walk away with your head held high.

Character

Good character is
the best insurance.

PROVERBS 11:6 MSG

You can't know the future—even what will happen an hour from now. So you do what you can to protect yourself and your family and then give your tomorrows to God. Some things are not within your control. Yet it is always within your power to grow spiritually. You can choose to pray, read God's Word, and listen to His Spirit's gentle direction. As you do, you'll learn who He is and He'll graciously develop love, patience, gentleness, and wisdom in you.

> Moral character makes
> for smooth traveling.
>
> PROVERBS 11:5 MSG

You may have heard this expression before: "Character counts!" Choosing to invest your time and energy in cultivating a sense of fairness, compassion, wisdom, and respect for life and God enhances your chances for contentment. How you live affects not only you but also those you love. Perhaps you lacked good role models as a child. This is your opportunity to start a new trend. What godly attribute would you like to develop this year? No doubt about it, you'll enjoy the benefits.

Charity

She opens her arms to the poor
and extends her hands to the needy.

PROVERBS 31:20 NIV

Family, home, job, church, friends, school,
personal and spiritual development—these
fill your days. No doubt, like many other
women, you find it difficult to become
involved in long-term charity projects.
Although you long to help, you only have
so much time, energy, and money to go
around. You can't do everything, but you can
do something. Ask God to help you establish
how, where, and when you can reach out to
the hurting people in your world.

Happy are those who are
kind to the poor.

PROVERBS 14:21 NRSV

A wise leader once said that you make a living by what you get—and you make a life by what you give. You receive a blessing when you give a blessing. As you develop wisdom, God expands your compassion for the poor. He smiles when you lovingly share with those who can't help themselves. And out of your gracious generosity springs joy. Your own life grows richer when you reach out in kindness to the disadvantaged.

Children

A refusal to correct
is a refusal to love;
love your children
by disciplining them.

PROVERBS 13:24 MSG

You want your children to make wise choices. You send them to the best school you can afford. You take them to church. You expect their teachers to instruct them well. And as their mother, you have the personal privilege of sharing what you've learned about living a God-honoring life. You show how much you love your children when you graciously tell and show them what is right and wrong in God's sight.

> Train up a child in
> the way he should go,
> and when he is old
> he will not depart from it.

PROVERBS 22:6 NKJV

Jesus promised that anyone who believes in Him will live forever. Paul wrote that we'll experience peace when we give our worries to God. Yet the pithy sayings in Proverbs aren't really promises. They're principles for wise living. One principle indicates that when your children are instructed and have seen that instruction modeled in your life, it becomes second nature to them. And when your children grow older, they will continue to make God-honoring choices.

Commitment

Commit your works to the LORD,
and your thoughts will
be established.

PROVERBS 16:3 NKJV

When you don't understand all that's happening and aren't certain what to do next, honor your initial commitment to God. Continue with what God has shown you in the light or in less-confusing times. Do what is in front of you to do—without retreating into an isolating fear-maze. Although you may not know what your long-term future holds, walk through the doors of opportunity that open each day. In time God will establish your thoughts and clarify your path.

Commit yourself to instruction;
listen carefully to words
of knowledge.

PROVERBS 23:12 NLT

As a wise woman, you avoid succumbing to victim mentality. You no longer believe that you have little or zero choice in life. You stop saying yes when you really mean no. You cease doing for others what they can do for themselves. Realizing that the other person has the right to say no, you feel comfortable asking for what you need anyway. You seek advice, gain knowledge, and remain committed to personal and spiritual growth. Congratulations, wise woman!

Communication

An open, face-to-face
meeting results in peace.
PROVERBS 10:10 MSG

Perhaps growing up you learned that it's more loving to avoid honest communication than to share what you really feel, think, or need. Maybe it was easier to blame—or relay messages through someone else rather than deliver them yourself. Now you notice this approach fails to bring the results you desire. Sharing directly and honestly while encouraging others to do the same allows peace to flow into your relationships. Ask God for help in developing this wise communication skill.

> As a tree gives fruit,
> healing words give life.
>
> PROVERBS 15:4 NCV

Sticks and stones may break my bones, but words will never hurt me." Perhaps you're familiar with this often-repeated phrase. But is it true? Research shows that vicious teasing or persistent shaming and bullying can cause low self-esteem and even depression. On the flip side, encouraging, kind words heal and uplift. Just as a well-watered tree produces nourishing fruit, you nurture others when you listen, reflect, and empower them with your words.

Conversation

Watch your words
and hold your tongue;
you'll save yourself a lot of grief.

PROVERBS 21:23 MSG

Some of you tend to say almost anything
that pops into your mind. This leads to
laughter and rollicking conversation. You're
the life of the party. Your quieter friends
may envy your boldness. Yet sometimes you
utter an excited comment and inadvertently
hurt someone and cause yourself grief. God
doesn't want to change your effervescent
personality. He's the one who made you—
and your more reserved friend. He only
wants to temper your thoughts and words to
grace others.

The wise measure their words.

PROVERBS 10:19 MSG

You measure the amount of sugar you add when making a cake. You measure the window frame when sewing a curtain. But have you measured your words lately? Too many sugary words may seem like flattery instead of genuine praise. Neglect to plan your comments before introducing a new concept at work and what you say may not fit. You don't have to be hypervigilant about your conversations, but it's wise to think before you speak. Ask God for direction.

Counsel

Without good direction,
people lose their way;
the more wise counsel you follow,
the better your chances.

PROVERBS 11:14 MSG

Have you ever thought you knew the way to
an appointment destination only to discover
you were driving in the opposite direction?
Frustrating, isn't it? Asking a reliable source
for directions to follow greatly reduces
your chances of ending up at an unwanted
destination. Likewise, it's a sensible idea
to pause and seek help when you feel lost
in a relationship, with your job, or in
your spiritual life. Following wise counsel
enhances your chances for fulfillment,
success, and growth.

> The heartfelt
> counsel of a friend
> is as sweet as
> perfume and incense.
>
> PROVERBS 27:9 NLT

Picture yourself walking through a forest filled with fresh-smelling pine trees, tending the fragrant rose bushes in your front yard, or strolling down the aisles of your favorite bath and body lotions store. Sweet aromas; pleasant thoughts. Just as sweet is the loving counsel of a trusted friend. You don't have to be the one always advising. You don't have to be the one continually on the receiving end either. Good friends give and receive advice from one another.

Creation

Who but God goes up to heaven
and comes back down?
Who holds the wind. . . ?
Who wraps up the oceans in
his cloak? Who has created
the whole wide world?

PROVERBS 30:4 NLT

Every thinking woman is responsible
for her conclusions concerning the origin
of our vast universe. Whether she insists
God does or does not exist, she develops a
belief system. Science invites you to view and
study life's extraordinary complexities, the
structural design inherent in each cell and
how it all works together so intentionally.
A wise woman like you will conclude that
instead of pushing God out of the picture,
this investigation pulls Him closer.

By wisdom the LORD laid the earth's foundations, by understanding he set the heavens in place; by his knowledge the deeps were divided, and the clouds let drop the dew.

PROVERBS 3:19–20 NIV

You may sometimes encounter people who don't know God as the all-powerful Creator. Perhaps you've been told by these people that evolution is the only intelligent way to believe and that religion should have no place in our educational system or in the study of science. Be kind, but refuse to be intimidated. You possess a deeper, more inspired wisdom that allows you to look beyond the smallness of the human mind and see the God behind it all.

Delight

A good person basks
in the delight of GOD.

PROVERBS 12:2 MSG

Don't you love it when a friend says, "It
was a delight to be with you"? You feel warm
inside just knowing that someone you like
likes you back. God likes you, too. Really. In
fact, He delights in you. You've been made
delightful in His sight through Jesus' death
and resurrection. You may already know that
God loves you. After all, that's His nature.
But remember, too, that He likes you—you
are His delight.

> Those who act faithfully
> are his delight.
>
> PROVERBS 12:22 NRSV

God can be trusted to follow through on His word. He consistently loves you, your family, and all His creation. Each day He rolls out the sun, gives the birds their song, waters the grass with dew, and encourages gravity to keep you grounded. Every gift God gives is wrapped in truth, grace, and honor. That's who He is. And He loves it when you faithfully reflect His character in everyday life. No doubt about it, He delights in you.

Diligence

Look at an ant. Watch it closely;
let it teach you. . . .
Nobody has to tell it what to do.
All summer it stores up food;
at harvest it stockpiles provisions.

PROVERBS 6:6–8 MSG

When you see a line of ants traveling across your kitchen counter, it's not really a welcome sight. Yet ants model a few worthwhile lessons about how to accomplish everyday tasks. First, ants self-motivate. They don't need someone to push them or direct their every step. Also, ants do the task at hand without procrastination. They diligently work until they've completed each job. What wise lesson will you take from the ant today?

Diligent work gets
a warm commendation.

PROVERBS 14:35 MSG

Perhaps when you've been job hunting,
you've voiced this question: "What do
employers really want?" If so, you've
probably heard something like this:
"Companies hire people who are depend-
able, positive, flexible, honest, self-
motivated, loyal, teachable, and willing to
work hard and smart." Sounds like what
wise King Solomon wrote about so long
ago. Wisdom starts with God and produces
credibility whether in the kitchen, office,
or serving at church. Remember, your
diligence never goes out of style.

Direction

The human mind plans the way,
but the Lord directs the steps.

PROVERBS 16:9 NRSV

Your carefully thought-through plans may not play out as you envisioned they would. Life isn't predictable. Certainly it's not perfect. But one thing is sure. God knows the way through the good and disappointing times. He guides your steps, bringing opportunities across your path that will shape your character and help you become the wise woman you long to be. Let God direct you. He knows the way. He is the absolute best trail guide you could ever have.

In all your ways
acknowledge Him, and
He shall direct your paths.

PROVERBS 3:6 NKJV

President Abraham Lincoln said that
the good thing about the future is that it
comes only one day at a time. That's a relief,
because if you had to determine up front
how you would live each moment of the rest
of your life, you would be. . .well, massively
overwhelmed! So right now ask God to
direct you today. Tomorrow you can do it
again. Your daily trust creates a lifetime of
purposeful living.

Discernment

The discerning heart
seeks knowledge.

PROVERBS 15:14 NIV

Some people confuse gullibility with
open-mindedness. But think for a moment.
Believing everything you're told could
make you a target for unscrupulous people.
God doesn't want you to be vulnerable to
wrongdoers. When you seek His wisdom,
He promises you a heart of discernment
that creates a desire to study and discover
the truth. That's when you will experience
lightbulbs of understanding lighting up your
heart and mind.

The wise in heart are called
discerning, and pleasant
words promote instruction.

PROVERBS 16:21 NIV

Discernment is the ability to distinguish between the genuine and the counterfeit. It's the power to grasp what doesn't make sense. When you develop a discerning heart, you enjoy music, art, and godly things with deeper insight, although you recognize you'll never understand everything perfectly all the time. You become ready to share the joy with others— not in an "I got it. You need it" way, but with empathy and gentleness. It's a process worth the journey.

Discipline

To learn, you must love discipline.
PROVERBS 12:1 NLT

Discipline. Sometimes this word summons memories of disapproving grade school teachers. But discipline isn't really about scolding and pointing out flaws. It's about learning and enjoying life. Discipline is a good thing—and self-discipline multiplies the advantage. It allows you the privilege of taking responsibility for your own growth. Don't you love the thought of accomplishing your long-held physical, mental, relational, and spiritual dreams? This week, partner with God to take a disciplined step toward reaching one of your goals.

> "Mark a life of discipline
> and live wisely."
>
> PROVERBS 8:33 MSG

As a wise woman with a heart for God, you listen to instruction, consider your options, and then make intentional plans to practice what you've learned. You're focused, but not driven. You discover methods that help you exercise, sleep, and eat well. Allowing time for surprises and spontaneous service, you schedule your calendar sensibly. You're also gentle with yourself when you make inevitable human mistakes, because you know God wants you to relax and enjoy your life with Him.

Discretion

Discretion will preserve you;
understanding will keep you.

PROVERBS 2:11 NKJV

Sometimes when a farmer wants to protect
his territory, he plants a thorny hedge
around the perimeter. He hopes it will
protect his land and possessions from harm.

Discretion—or the ability to meditate,
think, purpose, and plan—works like a
protective hedge in your life. Not only
does God provide you with wisdom and
instruction for making wise decisions,
but He helps you gain the resources
and knowledge needed for reasoning,
organizing, and implementing your future
plans.

As a ring of gold in a swine's snout,
so is a lovely woman who
lacks discretion.

PROVERBS 11:22 NKJV

For a little comic relief, picture a large, muddy sow with a shiny gold ring in her snout. Rather ridiculous, isn't it? And highly unlikely. It's just as ridiculous and unlikely for a beautiful woman of God—lovely from the inside out—to live her daily life without exercising discretion. It's just not going to happen. Although gaining wisdom is an ongoing process, be assured that as you grow, you'll learn practical skills for planning and purposing your life.

Empathy

Singing cheerful songs to a person
with a heavy heart is like taking
someone's coat in cold weather
or pouring vinegar in a wound.

PROVERBS 25:20 NLT

Perhaps you've noticed how uncomfortable
it feels to be with someone who just lost
her job or broke up with her boyfriend. You
want to help change her mood. But often the
most helpful thing you can do is empathize.
Listen. Agree that she hurts. Verify her
disappointment. It allows her to accept
herself so she can eventually move on—in
her own time. This releases you from trying
to come up with the perfect cheerful words
to say.

> The person who shuns
> the bitter moments of
> friends will be an outsider
> at their celebrations.
>
> PROVERBS 14:10 MSG

You can't predict what will happen next year or even one hour from now. Sometimes circumstances bring happy moments. Other times you get news that rocks your world. When you feel sad or mistreated, you'd rather someone empathize than discount your reality. If friends disregard your pain often enough, you'll probably hesitate to share much else with them, even your joy-filled times. God wants you and your friends to be compassionate with one another whether times are sad or happy.

Encouragement

The words of the godly
encourage many.

PROVERBS 10:21 NLT

Everyone needs encouragement. Your
best friend needs it. Your son and daughter
need it. Your pastor needs it. So does your
sister. Your boss needs it. The deliveryman
needs it. If you're married, your spouse
needs it—even though he may not act like
he does. And what about you? Do you crave
some encouragement today? It's okay to
verbalize your desire, just as it's good to
encourage others with your words. Mutual
encouragement makes the world a richer
place.

Wise words satisfy like a good meal.
PROVERBS 18:20 NLT

Think of your favorite meal. It might be a white-tablecloth dinner of grilled salmon or steak. Or a casual setting with hamburger and french fries. Maybe vegetarian fare is your style. Whatever you prefer, it's a satisfying experience when you see, smell, and taste your favorite feast. Likewise, encouraging words of approval, support, gratitude, hope, and commendation—mixed with supportive actions—satisfy the soul. . .yours and the souls of your loved ones. How will you encourage someone today?

Equality

The rich and the poor
shake hands as equals—
God made them both!

PROVERBS 22:2 MSG

Intelligent men and women through the
ages have insisted that all people are created
equal. American leaders Thomas Jefferson,
Elizabeth Cady Stanton, and Abraham
Lincoln are a few. Yet long before they spoke
about equality, the Bible included similar
sentiments. God is the creator of all human
beings whether they are rich, poor, dark,
light, quick, or slow. You have the right to
breathe, think, act, and live freely—as does
the woman living 1,000 miles from you.

The poor and the
oppressor have this in common:
the Lord gives light to the
eyes of both.

PROVERBS 29:13 NRSV

Someone once said, "You and I are equal
with the human race. No better than. No less
than." When we believe this, it changes our
lives. We grow to work, play, love, and serve
with greater love, patience, and acceptance.
No person is on this earth to "lord it over"
another. Neither is one here to be a doormat
for someone else. As God does for each
individual, He gives you eyes to see others as
your equals.

Expectations

A good woman is hard to find,
and worth far more
than diamonds.

PROVERBS 31:10 MSG

God created men and women with the capacity to reason, feel, choose, plan, and execute. After designing the first male and female and putting them in charge of His creation, He declared it all "very good." Yet sometimes women grade themselves by measurements other than God's, consequently setting unrealistic standards for themselves. Be gentle with yourself today. You're worth far more than precious jewels.

Unrelenting disappointment leaves you heartsick, but a sudden good break can turn life around.

PROVERBS 13:12 MSG

I should. . ." "He must. . ." "I have to. . ." When your self-chatter repeatedly includes these phrases, you may believe the lie that people, projects, and circumstances have the ability to be perfect. Expecting perfection causes everyone and everything in your life to become a continual disappointment. It's better to accept the truth: People, actions, and situations don't have the ability to be constantly flawless on earth. Only God is perfect. Isn't that a relief?

Faith

Trust God from the bottom
of your heart; don't try to
figure out everything on your own.
PROVERBS 3:5 MSG

Doubts come. They're part of your
inherent humanness. God knows that.
Things have happened to you that make
trusting Him seem foolish. It can feel like
the ultimate paradox to release what you've
worked so hard to cultivate. Yet God loves
you and wants to ease your fear and anxiety.
Picture this: unclenching the fist of your
heart and releasing the problems you've
tried relentlessly to figure out on your own.
You don't have to do life alone. God
waits patiently.

Whoever trusts in
the Lord will be enriched.

PROVERBS 28:25 NRSV

What is faith, anyway? Is it the church you attend? The creed you follow? In part, but it's deeper than that. Faith involves confidence in God's ability to finish what He started in you, trusting He will do what you can't figure out. Personal faith means loosening your grip on your family, job, circumstances, and future. You let go, not into the unknown universe, but to your loving Father. And in this letting go you find freedom and life.

Family

The integrity of good people
creates a safe place for living.

PROVERBS 14:32 MSG

Whatever your role—sister, aunt, mother, daughter, spouse—you enjoy sharing good times with those you love. You also want them to feel comfortable approaching you with their disappointments. But how? A wise woman knows that others feel safe with someone who's the same on the inside as she is on the outside—one who listens first and then talks. Ask God to help you create a warm and safe place for your family to live and share.

Old people are proud of their
grandchildren, and children
are proud of their parents.

PROVERBS 17:6 NCV

Families are God's idea. He created the
concept of a loving unit—mother, father, and
children—growing and learning together
through challenges, disappointments,
celebrations, moves, births, deaths, and
surprises. There's no other group quite like
the family. It has been said that you didn't
choose your parents or your siblings, and it's
true. But God is pleased when you support
one another, relishing each other's gifts,
dreams, and accomplishments with pride.
Invite God to love your family through you.

Fear of the Lord

The fear of the Lord is the beginning of wisdom.

PROVERBS 9:10 NRSV

Fear blocks intimacy. It can hinder you from trying new things and cause you to obsess about finances or health. Fear threatens your contentment—even when you don't want it to. You want to be wise, free from fear. Then you read: "The fear of the Lord is the beginning of wisdom." Must you fear God, too? Yet, to "fear" God means to respect and reverence Him with deepest adoration. When you do, everyday fear begins to fade and wisdom flourishes.

Fear of the LORD is the foundation of true knowledge.

PROVERBS 1:7 NLT

Building a house means making critical decisions about subcontractors, materials, design elements, and more. Ask any builder and you'll discover that constructing the foundation is one of the most important tasks, because if it's not properly laid, the entire edifice will be unstable. Likewise, as you develop a life of wisdom, you'll want to lay a strong foundation based on your faith in God. As you honor and trust Him, every area of your life will be built on this strength.

Finances

Whoever makes deals
with strangers is sure to get burned;
if you keep a cool head,
you'll avoid rash bargains.

PROVERBS 11:15 MSG

Whether the economy is good or bad, promises of easy success flash across your television screen, pop up during online searches, and arrive in both your e-mail and snail-mail boxes. It's tempting to hop on board to get the best deal before it's too late. Yet God's wisdom instructs you to be thorough and check out the people behind the "good deals" before signing on. God wants to protect you financially.

Don't wear yourself out
trying to get rich;
be wise enough to control yourself.

PROVERBS 23:4 NCV

With your income, you probably buy groceries, pay your mortgage, clothe and educate your children, decorate your home, and give to others. When you don't have adequate finances, you feel the loss. Yet it's easy to try too hard to accumulate wealth. If you overwork, you'll neglect your health, loved ones, and God, and you'll end up exhausted. But you don't have to live this way. You can learn to balance your life, control your resources, and enjoy what you have.

Friendship

Whoever walks with
the wise becomes wise.
PROVERBS 13:20 NRSV

Isn't it amazing how diverse friendships
can be? You may have friends for different
seasons of your life or friends with whom
you share a particular interest, friends
you've had forever, and friends you've just
met. It's essential, though, that you include
those who are wise in your circle of friends.
Spending time with people who have sound
judgment will help you stay clear-headed
and moving in the direction of a blessing-
filled life.

A friend loves
at all times.

PROVERBS 17:17 NRSV

Having a loving friend makes you feel rich
even when you don't have this month's rent
money. When your child gets picked up by
the police, a true friend hangs in there with
you. She cries when your mother dies—and
stays in touch when you move away. A loyal
friend's hug reassures you that your public
blunder wasn't the end of the world. Today,
thank a friend for her constant love.

Future

Always respect the Lord.
Then you will have
hope for the future.

PROVERBS 23:17–18 NCV

Even for wise women of God, the future sometimes appears blurry. What do you do when circumstances change? Plans don't work out like you thought they would? You lose something you cherish? There are no cookie-cutter answers. Yet as a woman with a heart for God, you can pause and remember when God has helped you in the past. You might even write these memories down. Now choose to let these previous times give you hope for what you'll face tomorrow.

The drippings of the honeycomb
are sweet to your taste. Know
that wisdom is such to your soul;
if you find it, you will find a future.

PROVERBS 24:13–14 NRSV

Some experts say that honey is a miracle food. It rarely spoils, contains no fat or cholesterol, and helps burn fats while you sleep. Yet it's most known for sweetness. Even thinking about honey-drizzled desserts makes your taste buds salivate in anticipation. Like honey is to your taste, wisdom—that unique understanding, knowledge, and insight about all the various aspects of life—is to your soul. No wonder gaining God's wisdom gives you hope for the future.

Generosity

A quietly given gift soothes
an irritable person; a heartfelt
present cools a hot temper.

PROVERBS 21:14 MSG

A knee-jerk reaction to an irritable clerk is to snap back. When a friend shoots an angry remark your direction, you may want to retaliate. However, when you offer the gift of a quiet response or understanding word, your generous act can defuse the tension. Even a gift of time or money can make a positive difference. Offer homemade cookies, lunch out, to take out the trash, or help with another project. Your quietly given gift can cool a heated situation.

The world of the
generous gets
larger and larger.

PROVERBS 11:24 MSG

Stories about celebrities' lifestyles splash
across the magazine covers at grocery
checkouts. Television news shows and
Internet sites follow their daily behavior and
activities. Some make positive contributions
to society. But you don't have to be a well-
paid star to be generous. Success isn't
calculated by dollars—it's calculated by who
you are and what you willingly contribute.
Your inner and outer worlds expand
when you give generously from your
personal storehouse.

Gentleness

A woman of gentle grace
gets respect.

PROVERBS 11:16 MSG

Perhaps you've heard your local news reporter deliver Friday night's weather report and mention that the forecast includes balmy temperatures and gentle breezes. "So go outside and enjoy your weekend," she might add. Technically, a gentle breeze means a wind with a speed of eight to twelve miles per hour. Just enough to refresh without blowing things around. Now imagine gracefully traveling through your days at the speed of a gentle breeze, showing gentleness to yourself and others. Lovely thought, isn't it?

A gentle answer turns away wrath.

PROVERBS 15:1 NIV

God invites you to come to Him with your daily irritations and angst. He's not threatening you with ultimatums or put-downs if you don't. Instead He waits and promises to listen even when you're mad at yourself for falling off your diet or yelling at your kids or not making your deadline at work. May His gentleness encourage you to practice patience with yourself and others, thereby silencing the anger bully and making room for peace.

God

*God's blessing makes life rich;
nothing we do can improve on God.*

PROVERBS 10:22 MSG

God is always the same, yet never boring.
He's continuously good, creative, kind,
compassionate, and timely. He protects,
loves, and guides you, your family,
neighbors, pastor, and those missionary
friends twelve flight hours away. Every
morning He's right beside you. He never
walks out when you're talking to Him.
Nothing you do can make God any better
than He is. He rules the universe but
knows what you're planning at 4:00 p.m.
tomorrow. For exciting life adventures,
partner with Him.

> GOD is in charge of
> human life, watching
> and examining us
> inside and out.
>
> PROVERBS 20:27 MSG

Pop stars sing tunes that bemoan how lovers and friends don't take time to really know one another. We hear lyrics similar to "He only talks about himself. . . ." "She left before we bonded. . . ." "He doesn't really know me. . . ."

People desire intimacy. So if you're like most folks, you want your loved ones to ask about your dreams, listen, and love you in spite of and because of what they hear. God does. He delights in knowing you inside and out.

Goodness

So you may walk in
the way of goodness...

PROVERBS 2:20 NKJV

Archbishop Desmond Tutu, a Nobel Peace
Prize recipient from South Africa said, "The
world is hungry for goodness." With so
much immorality, power-mongering, and
terrorism in the world, people long for the
good. But what does that mean? Goodness
is a basket full of rich characteristics that
include excellence, virtue, beauty, joy,
kindness, and wisdom. Genuine goodness
counteracts moral evil. Sounds like a partial
definition of God, doesn't it? Ask God to
help you share His goodness with your
world.

Your generosity will surprise
him with goodness,
and GOD will look after you.
PROVERBS 25:22 MSG

Heap coals of fire upon his head." You've probably heard this line before. It originated from the wisest man who ever lived. "If your enemy is hungry, give him food to eat; if he is thirsty, give him water to drink," wrote King Solomon. "In doing this, you will heap burning coals on his head." It's opposite of how you might want to treat a stubborn foe. Yet your generous response will shock him with goodness and reflect God's grace.

Grace

Keep sound wisdom and
discretion; so they will be life
to your soul and grace to your neck.

PROVERBS 3:21–22 NKJV

Would you like to be less self-critical?
Reduce the silent inner nit-picking? It's
possible and it happens as you develop
wisdom, discretion, and grace in the midst
of your humanness. As you accept God's
unmerited love through His Son, Jesus,
realize that He grants you extra time to learn
and grow and that He genuinely cares about
your emotional, spiritual, and physical
needs. Breathing in God's grace allows you
to exhale that same grace onto others.

A mean person gets
paid back in meanness,
a gracious person in grace.

PROVERBS 14:14 MSG

As you become a grace-full person, the
judgmental, overachieving, demanding
attitudes will shrink. You'll notice you're
breathing deeply, enjoying life, and feeling
more grateful and generous—not perfectly
24/7 (you're still human!), but increasingly.
You won't suddenly be the ultimate expert
on grace, yet you'll desire more—for
yourself, your loved ones, and those you
hardly know. When you enjoy being gracious
at home, at work, and everywhere you
go, it comes back to you like a contagious
blessing.

Gratitude

Ears to hear and eyes to see—
both are gifts from the LORD.

PROVERBS 20:12 NLT

Everything you have is a gift from God:
the air you breathe, the sunset you enjoy,
the rain that nourishes your garden, your
work, love of family and friends, your taste
buds, freedom, music, a bird's song, art, the
creativity to design. All things are God's,
and He shares them with you, to bring you
pleasure. What are you grateful for today?
Pause for a moment and thank Him for all
His gifts.

Honor God with everything you own;
give him the first and the best.
Your barns will burst.

PROVERBS 3:9–10 MSG

You make a wise choice when you honor God with your wealth—whether it is great wealth (by society's standards) or only a little. God blesses you when you share what you have. Forget about the idea that you need to overwork, overdo, and keep it up 24/7 in order to please God. That's your inner bully speaking and not our heavenly Father. Silence the inner tyrant by naming what you're thankful for. Gratitude changes your focus.

Growth

The LORD gives wisdom;
from his mouth come knowledge
and understanding; he stores up
sound wisdom for the upright; he is a
shield to those who walk in integrity.

PROVERBS 2:6–8 ESV

God is not stingy. He willingly and liberally
shares His love, patience, instruction, and
wisdom with you. Identify a characteristic
or attribute you want to cultivate and
share your desire with God and another
trustworthy person. Ask God to help you
clarify your next step and then seek to learn
as much as you can about it. God wants to
be your guide on this daily adventure of
learning, changing, and growing.

The wise are mightier
than the strong, and
those with knowledge grow
stronger and stronger.

PROVERBS 24:5 NLT

King Solomon, author of most of the pithy sayings in Proverbs, didn't write a handbook for success, but an instruction manual for living a wise and meaningful life. No matter what the level of your academic education, you can be a knowledgeable, disciplined, perceptive, and discerning woman. When you understand that it is your choice how you live—and you decide to trust God—then you are set free to grow and become who God designed you to be.

Health

A cheerful look brings joy
to the heart; good news
makes for good health.

PROVERBS 15:30 NLT

Medical experts indicate that it does matter whether you see the proverbial glass half empty or half full. Many believe that positive thinking leads to lower rates of depression, increased life span, and reduced risk of death from heart disease. Consequently, health professionals urge their patients to cultivate optimistic attitudes. Guess what? God recommends this also. Search for the good news in your life today. Make a list and display it where you'll see it often.

A reliable messenger
brings healing.

PROVERBS 13:17 NLT

Just because you look for the good side of your circumstances doesn't mean that you deny reality. Sometimes problems exist that are impossible to ignore. To continue looking the other way is foolish. It's not wise or healthy to ignore addiction, abuse, signs of depression, or unpleasant medical symptoms. When a reliable person speaks up courageously, healing can begin. Maybe that person is you.

Heart

Tune your ears to wisdom,
and concentrate on understanding.
Cry out for insight, and
ask for understanding.

PROVERBS 2:2–3 NLT

Past generations seemed to emphasize the non-emotional life approach. If you could see something with your physical eyes, prove it through scientific research, or touch it with your hands, it was considered valid. Recently there's been a shift to the "spiritual" side of human existence. But through it all, God hasn't changed. He's always cared about your heart and your intellect. Turn your thoughts and emotions over to God, asking Him for the understanding to make wise heartfelt decisions in your everyday circumstances.

> Trust in the LORD
> with all your heart.
>
> PROVERBS 3:5 NKJV

Singing about God in church, saying
mealtime grace, attending Sunday school,
and giving generously to the poor are
worthwhile, God-honoring activities. Yet
these good behaviors will never replace a
genuine relationship with God. He longs to
interact with you on a personal level. That's
why God went to the trouble of sending
His Son Jesus to earth to give His life for
you. When you trust God wholeheartedly,
nothing stands between you and Him. Isn't
that great news?

Helping

Do not withhold good from those
to whom it is due, when it is in the
power of your hand to do so.

PROVERBS 3:27 NKJV

The Bible provides a great basis for Sunday
sermons about God and His plans. Yet
it also includes nitty-gritty advice about
acquiring people skills and cultivating a
habit of bigheartedness. You can't assist
everyone in this hurting world, but you can
help in everyday ways—perhaps by carrying
an elderly friend's heavy package, allowing
a waiting driver into your lane, sharing
pro bono business advice, or comforting
a crying child. Helping is your personal
privilege—and it's doable.

Rescue the perishing;
don't hesitate to step in and help.

PROVERBS 24:11 MSG

When you reach out to pray, support, and act on behalf of those who cannot help themselves, you reflect God's loving concern for all people. However, walking beyond your own comfort to advocate for those suffering injustice, abuse, or inadequacy is not always easy. When do you step in? How do you help? You can't do it all. Yet you can ask God for direction and then step up courageously as He touches your heart with someone's need.

Home

Through wisdom a house is built,
and by understanding it
is established; by knowledge
the rooms are filled with
all precious and pleasant riches.

PROVERBS 24:3–4 NKJV

Perhaps you're frustrated that your home isn't like you pictured it would be. Your spouse and children didn't turn out as you dreamed they would. Disappointment tugs at you. But nothing and no one is perfect here on this earth. Your loved ones have good and bad days, just like you do. That's okay, because if your home and family were flawless, you wouldn't need God. Trusting and gaining His understanding fills your heart and home with joy, love, and acceptance.

> A wise woman
> strengthens her family.
>
> PROVERBS 14:1 NCV

Maybe you can't wield a sledgehammer all afternoon. Perhaps you can't win the marathon year after year. Maybe you don't have stamina to sing oratorios or write annual bestselling books. But you are strong. As you seek God's wisdom, knowledge, and discernment, your inner strength increases. That's great news, because you've been given a unique job: the privilege of building and strengthening your home. Whether you have a family of one, two, five, or ten, God partners with you.

Honesty

The Lord wants honest
balances and scales.

PROVERBS 16:11 NCV

God values truth-telling. Years ago people used stone weights on scales to determine the measurements of the products they sold. Dishonest store owners labeled the stones incorrectly to pad their profits. Dishonesty saddened God then as it does now. God loves for His children to be honest. Yet sometimes it seems more comfortable to avoid the truth if it isn't to your advantage. Being honest with your personal and professional dealings and relationships takes God-given courage—and it's incredibly freeing.

Honest people are relaxed
and confident, bold as lions.

PROVERBS 28:1 MSG

Throughout history women have been admired for their strength, courage, and confidence. Jesus' mother, Mary, is no exception. Although she was a teenager and no doubt surprised when God called her to carry His Son, Jesus, she remained honest when it might have been easier to evade the truth. God calls you to be honest in your current circumstances, too. And in that honesty, you'll find strength as you trust that God has it all under control.

Humility

Don't assume that you know it all.
Run to God! . . .
Your body will glow with health,
your very bones will vibrate with life!

PROVERBS 3:7–8 MSG

It's unrealistic to think you can figure out everything and everyone—even though you're a capable woman and some say you have eyes in the back of your head! Seriously, it's just too much pressure to try to know it all month after month, year after year. The stress takes a toll on your health. So as a woman committed to making wise choices, you can release your need to know, turn your concerns over to God, and relax.

He. . .gives grace
to the humble.

PROVERBS 3:34 NIV

We love grace. It represents kindness, favor, and beauty. Who doesn't want these pleasant gifts? But humility? It's difficult to understand and tougher still to desire. Yet God says He honors humility. In part, this means seeing yourself as God sees you: imperfect and needy, but forgiven and freed from what weighs you down through the death of Jesus on the cross. You recognize that God is God and you are not, and this acknowledgement brings you back to grace.

Integrity

GOD. . .relishes integrity.

PROVERBS 11:20 MSG

God cares about integrity. He wants you to be the same inside as you appear outside. Some may think this integrity dilemma only shows up when someone pretends to love God but really doesn't. But there's a painful flip side that women encounter when they deeply desire God but live to please someone else instead. Thankfully, there's a cure. Courageously permit your heart to influence your actions, even when it's uncomfortable. God will help.

A hot furnace tests silver and gold, but the Lord tests hearts.

PROVERBS 17:3 NCV

Lord, show me who I am now and who I can become—the woman You had in mind when You created me." With this prayer, you begin the lifelong process of becoming you—learning your passions, gifts, talents, and God-given personality. You start to discover what holds you back and what you need to move forward. It starts in the heart. God investigates your heart and shares His findings with you. Together you create a heart of integrity.

Intentionality

She looks over a field
and buys it, then,
with money she's put aside,
plants a garden.

PROVERBS 31:16 MSG

You've heard it before: Be proactive.
But what does it mean? In part it means
to initiate wise change instead of merely
reacting to problems. For example, you set a
goal to eat healthier. You pray about it, make
a plan, research options, and visualize the
outcome. But that's not enough. You need to
act on your plan to see it come to fruition.
You and your goals are important to God.
Ask Him to help you act intentionally.

> It's the child he loves
> that GOD corrects;
> a father's delight is behind all this.
>
> PROVERBS 3:12 MSG

God delights in coaching you toward maturity. Just as a caring, patient human father does, He enjoys showing you new adventures, planning methods to help you learn, and watching you practice and gain confidence in your new skills. When He notices that you need direction, He corrects you—similar to what an earthly father does when he sees his child throw the softball improperly. God is intentional about training and encouraging you. Aren't you glad He loves you like that?

Joy

There is. . .joy for those
who promote peace.

PROVERBS 12:20 NIV

Doesn't it seem like someone is always promoting something? A new book. An updated diet. A time management program. An insurance policy. A charity opportunity. A miracle medicine. A new money-making system. The latest powerful vacuum cleaner. Any or all of these ideas may have merit. Yet for those who promote peace, harmony, well-being, and fulfillment, there's certain joy. God delights in you and you are privileged to share that delight-filled encouragement with others. Go ahead. Market a little joy today.

The hope of the righteous brings joy.
PROVERBS 10:28 ESV

There's an ongoing debate rumbling around: What's the difference between a Christian and a nonbeliever? Even those who don't follow Christ often agree the difference is hope: the sure expectation that God is on your side and you'll spend eternity with Him, no matter what happens during your earthly life. Beyond all the good deeds you can muster, you're made righteous in God's eyes by the gift of Christ's life, death, and resurrection. And that hope brings genuine joy.

Justice

Speak up for those who
cannot speak for themselves;
ensure justice for those
being crushed.

PROVERBS 31:8 NLT

When good people keep silent, injustice and abuse prevail. Remember the well-planned Nazi extermination of the Jews before World War II? Think of the many news stories detailing the tragic deaths of innocent children at the hands of their abusive parents. Results would be different if someone had successfully interceded. If you find it daunting to challenge bullies, you're not alone. It is intimidating. But may godly people everywhere join together and ask God for courage to follow His directive.

She opens her mouth with wisdom,
and the teaching of kindness
is on her tongue.

PROVERBS 31:26 NRSV

No matter what your season of life, you are influencing someone. In your job you may train others or greet clients on the phone or have lunch with coworkers. At home you interact with neighbors, your parents, your spouse, and your child. At church you may teach a class or sing in the choir. Perhaps you deal with teachers at school or live with peers in a retirement community. Whatever your interactions this week, add a little extra kindness.

Knowledge

Pay attention to my wisdom,
listen well to my words of insight,
that you may maintain discretion and
your lips may preserve knowledge.

PROVERBS 5:1–2 NIV

If you're somewhat confused about the difference between wisdom and knowledge, you're not alone. Many women doubt they'll ever be truly wise (or successful) because they don't have the credentials that others do. Sometimes they retreat and miss the rewards of living as the women God created them to be. Knowledge accumulates information—and that's valuable. Wisdom combines your heart knowledge, experience, and gifts, then moves past knowing to doing what is right—and that's possible when you partner with God.

> For giving prudence
> to the simple, knowledge
> and discretion to the young—let the
> wise listen and add to their learning,
> and let the discerning get guidance.
>
> PROVERBS 1:4–5 NIV

God loves helping you grow wise. He also loves seeing you learn new things and adding to your inner pool of knowledge. The more discerning you become, the more you are able to help others who need understanding and wisdom to make important choices that will impact their lives. God loves you so much, and He is pleased with you for seeking to be a wiser and more knowledgeable woman, a woman He can use to bless others.

Laughter

A cheerful heart is a good medicine.

PROVERBS 17:22 NRSV

The world is filled with trouble, stress, and responsibility. It can be pretty tough at times to keep your sense of humor and your positive perspective. Laughter breaks the tension and allows your body and soul to take a deep, healing breath. It lifts you up when everything around you is pulling you down. No matter what your circumstances, look for opportunities to laugh, and if you don't find any, create some of your own.

A glad heart makes
a cheerful countenance.

PROVERBS 15:13 NRSV

Grab the latest women's magazines from the rack at your local grocery checkout. After browsing the articles and ads, you may notice that their brand of beauty comes from wearing this season's lip gloss shades, lengthening your eyelashes, finding the perfect blush, and concealing all age spots. The products that promise all this may make you look more polished, but your entire expression changes when you have a happy heart—one that easily gives way to smiles, gratitude, and laughter.

Leadership

Good leadership is a channel
of water controlled by GOD;
he directs it to whatever
ends he chooses.

PROVERBS 21:1 MSG

You are a leader. Maybe you don't think
so, but you are. Someone looks up to you
and would like your support, advice, and
encouragement. Perhaps you doubt your
ability to lead well. Still, you long to live and
inspire others with a sincere heart—with
intentionality, wisdom, and grace. Be
encouraged, because God loves to guide you.
Partner with Him and be assured that He's
working in you to influence others for good.

Love and truth form
a good leader;
sound leadership is founded
on loving integrity.

PROVERBS 20:28 MSG

Intentional leaders work at becoming proactive in life and ministry. But perhaps you wonder what it means to be *on purpose* or *intentional*. Being *unintentional* is being haphazard about your personal and spiritual growth and your ministry deeds—merely reacting to whatever need comes along. You'll find fulfillment in your leadership roles when you seek God's wise direction about your unique gifting, serving with integrity, and loving with a transformed heart.

Legacy

The Fear-of-God builds up
confidence, and makes
a world safe for your children.

PROVERBS 14:26 MSG

The family that prays together stays together." You may have heard—and believed—this adage. You take your children to church and encourage them to listen to their teachers and to follow God's directives. That's good, but the greatest thing you can do for them is face your own wrong before God, accept Jesus as God's provision for your need, and grow spiritually. As they see you trust God, it will inspire them to do the same.

The godly walk with integrity;
blessed are their children
who follow them.

PROVERBS 20:7 NLT

You probably want your children to have what you didn't have growing up, to learn what you didn't learn, to experience what you didn't experience, and to make wise choices. So you correct their behavior and help them learn to solve their own problems. Although telling them to be honest and good is important, showing and modeling integrity and transformation is key. Your loving acceptance and example will bless them and leave a rich legacy far beyond your earthly years.

Life

The Fear-of-God
expands your life.
PROVERBS 10:27 MSG

People seem hungry for something to give their lives meaning. If you listen to current hit songs, you'd think that meaning comes from having another human being love you more than anyone else in the world. But what happens when that love interest gets mad, disappoints you, or finds someone else? Life becomes a drag. Only developing a relationship with God through Jesus Christ will fill that hole in your heart. Let Him give your life fresh meaning.

Respect for the Lord
gives life.
It is like a fountain that
can save people from death.

PROVERBS 14:27 NCV

The more you grow to respect God, the more you appreciate His daily gifts and enjoy being with Him. Maybe you pause more often to ask Him for His advice. You know your life is richer now (and will be for eternity) because you believe that Jesus, God's Son, gave His life for you. Even though you don't understand it all, you feel like there's a fresh stream of water flowing through your heart, giving you new life.

Listening

Spouting off before listening to the
facts is both shameful and foolish.

PROVERBS 18:13 NLT

How do you feel when someone listens
to you without telling you what to do?
Research indicates that this type of
interaction helps people find their own
answers and take intentional action. Most
women (men and children, too) long to be
heard and understood. Yet it's difficult to
hear another's bewilderment, pain, or joy
when you interject your own thoughts and
opinions. You may long to provide solutions,
but it's wise to listen to the whole story
before giving advice. Listening encourages
mutual growth.

Wise men and women
are always learning,
always listening for fresh insights.

PROVERBS 18:15 MSG

Listening offers a win/win scenario for relationships—at home, work, church, or in the neighborhood. However, it's common to sometimes focus on the chatter in your own head while another person is talking. A wise woman learns to concentrate on the other person and listen for the message and reality beneath the content of a person's words. When you listen on a deeper level, you gain rich insights about life, others, yourself, and God.

Marriage

Let your wife be a fountain
of blessing for you.
Rejoice in the wife of your youth.

PROVERBS 5:18 NLT

Marriage involves two people—a man and a woman. You both share responsibility for the success, happiness, and godliness of your union. As a wise woman, you can't make a man love and honor you. Neither will a wise man demand you to love and respect him. Wisdom recommends that as husband and wife, you cherish one another, finding blessing in each other above all others, remaining sexually and emotionally faithful throughout your lives together.

> A virtuous and capable
> wife. . .is more precious
> than rubies. Her husband can trust
> her, and she will greatly enrich his
> life. She brings him good, not harm.

PROVERBS 31:10–12 NLT

If you're a wife, God wants you to appreciate the good things your husband does for you, your family, and friends. God desires that you value your husband's ideas and that he values yours. As a committed follower of Christ, you don't live through your husband, but with him. You wisely allow your husband to take responsibility for his own decisions and growth, thus he trusts you. As you work together, you both experience a joy that is contagious.

Mercy

Guilt is banished through
love and truth.

PROVERBS 16:6 MSG

We have a problem. You can sense it when you try to be good and can't—at least not for long. You can feel it when patience eludes you. Sometimes you panic as fear threatens your fledgling faith. Consequently you know. We know. God is perfect; we aren't. But God banishes the weight of our guilt with His love exhibited in Jesus, who said, "I am the Truth." Then you believe and are free.

You can't whitewash your sins
and get by with it; you find mercy
by admitting and leaving them.

PROVERBS 28:13 MSG

Have you ever wondered what sin includes? Some say you sin when you don't act in the way they believe you should, or when you fail to go to church several times a week. Yet God says sin is living like He doesn't matter. We can't pretend we haven't treated God this way at times. It's the human predicament. So you can stop trying to be what you aren't, admit your need, and find mercy. Now isn't that blessed relief?

Money

Better is a dry morsel
with quiet than a house
full of feasting with strife.

PROVERBS 17:1 NRSV

Spending money allows you to make positive differences at home, in your city, and the world. You can provide opportunities for education, enhance enjoyment of the arts, build beautiful homes, feed hungry children, and fund worthwhile projects. In your personal life money helps you pay rent, buy groceries, heat your home, provide your children with music lessons, and secure health coverage. Yet money doesn't buy harmony, tranquillity, or unity. First seek wisdom and then spend with discernment.

A thick bankroll is
no help when life falls
apart, but a principled life
can stand up to the worst.

PROVERBS 11:4 MSG

How much does she make? Where does he live? What are they worth? Perhaps you've heard questions like these. Our culture values money and those who accumulate it. People who have "made it financially" hold great influence. It's understandable, for money can do a lot. Yet a thick bankroll doesn't guarantee emotional, mental, or spiritual strength when trouble comes. Your wise life with God will stand secure when money lets you down. And with that you can rest easier.

Nature

"God stretched out
Earth's Horizons, and tended
to the minute details of Soil and
Weather, and set Sky firmly in place."

PROVERBS 8:26–27 MSG

Picture yourself standing on a cliff gazing down on the crashing waves. Close your eyes and imagine walking in the mountains among the tall trees. Can you smell the pine? Hear the wind through the leaves? Now, close this book, go outside, and stare at the sky. Blue? Cloudy? Rainy? Whatever you find, it's all God's. All this loveliness is the work of His hands. He created it for His glory and your delight. So go and enjoy!

I'll never understand—how an
eagle flies so high in the sky,
how a snake glides over a rock,
how a ship navigates the ocean.

PROVERBS 30:18–19 MSG

Have you ever watched a documentary on birds, reptiles, or the deep? Fascinating, isn't it? You may learn that an eagle's eyesight is five or six times sharper than a human's. Or that snakes use their muscles and scales to push off bumpy surfaces but can't move on glass at all. Or that colorful species of fish exist miles below the ocean's surface. God designed every creature. You don't have to understand it all to worship your Creator.

Obedience

Follow my advice. . .
always treasure my commands.
Obey my commands and live!
Guard my instructions as
you guard your own eyes.

PROVERBS 7:1–2 NLT

Obedience is not a popular word today. If you're like many adult women, you don't want someone telling you what to do and who to be. You dread being quashed by another's demands. Yet when God asks you to obey His directives, He's liberating you. His guidelines help you take care of your soul. Follow Him to become the best you can be.

> Those who obey the
> commands protect themselves.
>
> PROVERBS 19:16 NCV

You are learning to treat yourself well. You don't make a practice of behaving in self-destructive ways, nor do you sabotage your relationships or your finances. Recognizing God's authority, you choose to follow His instructions. Like all human beings, you sometimes make mistakes; but you think them through, remedy what you can, and forgive yourself. You know that when you obey God and grow, you actually are protecting yourself from harm. In this you can find comfort and joy.

Options

The soul of the diligent
is richly supplied.

PROVERBS 13:4 ESV

I have no choice in the matter." Perhaps you've uttered these words when facing a difficult decision. If so, you've probably felt the trapped sensation that accompanies this misbelief. The truth is, you do have choices. You can ask questions, research your options, consider the pros and cons, and then make a reasonable choice based on the knowledge you have at the time. By your own diligent action, that boxed-in feeling will subside and you'll enjoy new freedom.

The first speech in a court case
is always convincing—until the
cross-examination starts!
You may have to draw straws when
faced with a tough decision.

PROVERBS 18:17–18 MSG

What you believe about a situation or person affects how you feel and what you do. That's good, because by altering your belief to correctly reflect reality, you can change how you feel and transform your follow-up action. Consequently, it's wise to investigate both sides of an issue or opportunity. Listen, see the merit in each option, and your judgmental attitudes will fade. You'll realize that several choices are acceptable and no one has the perfect answer all the time.

Patience

Patient persistence
pierces through indifference;
gentle speech breaks
down rigid defenses.

PROVERBS 25:15 MSG

Microwave dinners, e-mails and Twitter posts on your cell phone, 24/7 news channels, instant messaging. We're not used to waiting for much. But when it comes to relationships, we really need patience. You can't change someone else. You can only adjust your own attitudes and behavior. But positive change takes time, whether it is you or the other person who decides to change. Be encouraged, though. Patience and persistence will pay off in the long run.

> Do not boast about
> tomorrow, for you do
> not know what a day may bring forth.
>
> PROVERBS 27:1 NIV

Remember when you were a little girl,
looking forward to your family's summer
vacation? You wanted to go now. Mother
said, "Be patient." You couldn't wait for the
next day to arrive. Living one day at a time
is how you finally made it to your much-
anticipated holiday. Practicing patience
is like that. It's just one step at a time. You
don't know exactly what tomorrow will be
like. You have to live today first. So make the
most of it!

Peace

A heart at peace
gives life to the body.

PROVERBS 14:30 NIV

You are an exquisitely made woman.
Your body affects your mind, your
mind influences your emotions, your
emotions impact your beliefs and decisions,
and in turn, your choices affect your body.
God made you this way. He expects you
to value your body, mind, and emotions
because your fluctuating hormones and
chemical levels inevitably influence the
way you think, feel, and react. Ask God
for insight into practical and peace-filled
ways to manage your variable emotions and
thoughts.

When the ways of people please
the Lord, he causes even their
enemies to be at peace with them.

PROVERBS 16:7 NRSV

God loves us all the time, whether we make good or not-so-good choices. But just like any caring parent, God isn't pleased with our rebellious behavior. He instructs us about how to interact with others for our own benefit and satisfaction. It is a fact of life that when we choose to live by God's wise principles we experience peace—even with our enemies. Make it your goal to follow God's directives and enjoy peace with others.

People-Pleasing

An honest answer is
like a warm hug.

PROVERBS 24:26 MSG

Know anyone who pushes too hard to make
everything, or at least something, just right?
Perhaps you're the one who overachieves—
and you're tired. What motivates you to
continue this exhausting pattern? Maybe
you're trying to avoid someone's disapproval
by saying yes when you'd rather say no. God
wants to protect you from overwork and
burnout. Sometimes no is the most honest
answer you can give. It's like giving yourself
a warm hug.

> Being afraid of people
> can get you into trouble,
> but if you trust the Lord,
> you will be safe.
>
> PROVERBS 29:25 NCV

Your friend wants you to do one thing. Your husband suggests something else. Both their ideas are different than what your pastor asked of you. You feel torn. You're afraid that if you do what one would like, the other person will be displeased. You get that troubling, yet familiar feeling in the pit of your stomach. You can change your people-pleasing approach. God will help you get off this exhausting merry-go-round. Ask Him how to start the process and then trust His response.

Planning

Careful planning puts you ahead
in the long run; hurry and scurry
puts you further behind.

PROVERBS 21:5 MSG

When you follow God's lead in your life, is
planning really necessary? Perhaps you've
asked this question or heard someone voice
it. Planning may seem unspiritual—like
you're not really trusting God for your
immediate future. Yet when you avoid
making wise plans, often urgency takes
over. Then you feel pressure to hurry and
make it work. The good news is, careful
planning reduces stress in any role: home
manager, mother, volunteer, CEO, friend,
or employee.

Do your planning and prepare your
fields before building your house.

PROVERBS 24:27 NLT

God wants you to experience the many
benefits of wise planning. Through thoughtful preparation and open communication,
your team gets on the same page. Enthusiasm
and commitment increase. Responsibilities
and duties become clear. You know who does
what. Because your schedule makes sense,
that draining sense of overwhelming tasks
fades. You have space to deal with inevitable
surprises. You can measure the results.
And that creates a sense of satisfaction and
accomplishment. Now you're ready for the
next big step!

Pleasure

The Lord has made
everything for its purpose.
PROVERBS 16:4 NRSV

Pleasure isn't the key purpose of life, but it is one of God's perks to His children. Your five senses—hearing, seeing, touching, tasting, and smelling—are gifts from your loving Creator and evidences that He created you with the potential to enjoy yourself, others, and His creation. The next time you take a walk around your neighborhood, consciously listen, watch, touch, taste, and sniff your surroundings. Allow yourself to sink into the pleasure of being alive.

Living wisely brings pleasure to the sensible.

PROVERBS 10:23 NLT

God, the source of all wisdom, likes you in addition to loving you. He takes pleasure in you and delights in your company. And He longs for you to find pleasure in Him as well. God freely gives wisdom to those who seek and love Him, and He wants you to delight in His gift. So relax and enjoy playing and working today at your job, with your family, in your alone time, and with your friends.

Praise

Be zealous for the fear
of the LORD all the day.

PROVERBS 23:17 NKJV

There is no one like God. Never has been. Never will be. He keeps the earth balancing on its axis. He gives breath to every living creature. He promises eternal life to each believing soul. He cares. He provides. He protects. He comforts. He never makes a mistake. And that's just the beginning of who He is. God inspires awe, respect, and reverence, and this leads to spontaneous praise—all day long. Go ahead. Honor Him with your silent worship.

There is no wisdom, no insight,
no plan that can succeed
against the LORD.

PROVERBS 21:30 NIV

God is the ultimate question and the ultimate answer. No plan is more important than He is. His wisdom has no rival. All beneficial insight originates in Him. He created music and gives it as a loving gift to His children. He generously shares His creativity, knowledge, and joy with you, your family, your friends, your fellow church members, your coworkers, your heroes, and your government leaders. God will never stop giving, loving, saving, caring. Don't you want to praise Him?

Prayer

The name of the LORD
is a strong fortress;
the godly run to him and are safe.

PROVERBS 18:10 NLT

Stop. Pause. Breathe. Take a moment to contemplate how big God is. How He orchestrates nature by His power. That right now He is with you and with your friend across the ocean. How He never sleeps yet doesn't tire. Think how much He loves you. How He sent Jesus to prove that love. Let your heart run to Him. Sense His strong arms holding you. Pray, telling Him what you're feeling at this moment. You're safe with Him.

> The prayer of the
> upright is His delight.
>
> PROVERBS 15:8 NKJV

Perhaps you know what it feels like to be ignored or cut off when trying to talk to someone you care about. A spouse? Your father? Close friend? Boss? Child? It's hurtful—even maddening—to be disregarded. But God's not like that. He delights in listening to you. He knows you're not perfect. Still, He sees your desire to connect with Him. He looks at you through the sacrifice of His Son, Jesus. So drop any hesitancy. Go ahead. Pray.

Pride

The word *pride* has contrasting meanings. For example, when you hear a pastor say, "Pride alienates us from God," you may want to run in the opposite direction. Then someone introduces a respected Bible teacher with "She takes pride in what she's discovered and accomplished." So what's appropriate? Both. Although you don't wish to be arrogant, you do want to partner with God for your own growth and then accept the worthwhile results with dignity, gratitude, and celebration.

The wise listen to advice.

PROVERBS 12:15 NRSV

Negative pride is an enemy of the heart and can lead to exhaustion and burnout. It whispers, "I have a better idea, God." Sometimes it looks arrogantly brash. Other times, pride appears selfless and nice, but it tries too hard to fix everyone and play peacemaker at any cost. Both approaches leave little room for God's intervention, because pride has everything under control. Relief comes when we admit our need; listen to wise, gentle advice; and surrender it all to God.

Priorities

"Wisdom is best.
So get wisdom.
No matter what it costs,
get understanding."

PROVERBS 4:7 NIRV

Honoring God lays the foundation for building a life of wisdom. If you want to be wise, arrange your calendar to include time for God. You might have to say no to something in order to say yes to that Bible study or quiet time praying and reading God's Word or meeting with a spiritual mentor or attending worship service or keeping a spiritual journal. Though it may cost you, rearranging your priorities will help you gain wisdom.

Better a little with the fear of the LORD than great wealth with turmoil.

PROVERBS 15:16 NIV

If you listen to national news stories, you may notice that having lots of money doesn't guarantee contentment, perfect bodies, happy children, secure marriages, or stable investments. Although prosperity doesn't automatically lead to trouble, neither does it secure inner peace, health, or joy. In fact, reality indicates that problems abound when individuals strive solely for financial gain. Of much greater value is your personal relationship with the Creator God, the one who never changes and is worthy of your complete respect.

Protection

No need to panic over
alarms or surprises,
or predictions that doomsday's
just around the corner, because
GOD will be right there with you;
he'll keep you safe and sound.

PROVERBS 3:25–26 MSG

Everyone feels fearful at times. *What if
I lose my job? What if the terrorists strike
again? What if I get sick and can't take care
of my family?* None of us want these things
to happen. Yet when we focus on the what-
ifs, rationality and common sense often
go out the window. God, the wisdom giver,
is also your protector. He is right beside
you always. You can trust Him with this
moment—and with your future.

> "Every promise of God proves true; he protects everyone who runs to him for help."
>
> PROVERBS 30:5 MSG

God is true to His word. It's not in His nature to deceive or play games with you. He provided for the needs of Abraham, Moses, and Jesus' mother and earthly father. And He'll provide for your needs, too. God loves you a lot. He keeps all His promises to you. When you come to Him, telling Him about your concerns, asking for His protection, He meets you with open arms. With Him you are safe.

Prudence

The gullible believe anything
they're told; the prudent sift
and weigh every word.

PROVERBS 14:15 MSG

Try this toothpaste and you'll dazzle them with whiter teeth. Splash on this perfume and you'll have more dates. Follow these steps and double your income. Apply this lotion and say good-bye to crow's feet. But is it all true? Perhaps. Perhaps not. But you can find out. You don't have to fall victim to false promises and worry. The wise woman of God asks questions, researches her options, sifts through the maze, and then takes intentional action.

Wise realists plant their feet
on the ground.

PROVERBS 14:18 MSG

Your head's in the clouds!" If you heard
this as a child when you were just trying to
have fun, maybe you thought you should
stop dreaming, come down to earth, and be
boring. If you were praised for not keeping
your head in the clouds, you probably
learned to put your nose to the grindstone
and avoid pleasure. But being a wise realist
doesn't mean either extreme. You can make
thoughtful decisions about your reality and
still enjoy life.

Purity

Drink water from your
own well—share your love
only with your [husband.]

PROVERBS 5:15 NLT

Whether you're a wife or not, you've
probably noticed that infidelity is growing,
or at least people are talking about it more.
It's difficult to live in a culture where sexual
flirtation and innuendo has become just
another way to say hello. Contrary to what
movies, television, and the Internet may
suggest, the wisest approach to pleasing
the opposite sex is to stay true to yourself
and demonstrate respect. There you'll find
blessing—and joy.

> Mixed motives twist life
> into tangles; pure motives
> take you straight down the road.
>
> PROVERBS 21:8 MSG

Remember that game of Twister you used to play? Your arms and legs got twisted up with themselves and everyone else's. So you got confused and couldn't tell where to go next. Maybe that's how you feel about your life journey. If so, ask yourself: *What do I really want? Who or what am I doing this for?* Answering these questions helps you start over with pure motives, leaving any hidden agendas behind.

Purpose

"Are you confused about life,
don't know what's going on?
Come with me. . . . Leave your
impoverished confusion and live!
Walk up the street to
a life with meaning."

PROVERBS 9:4–6 MSG

God isn't put off by your confusion. Tell Him how you're feeling and what you're perplexed about—even if it doesn't make sense to you. He will give you purpose and meaning as you become more acquainted with His wise direction. You don't have to wait until you understand what your problems are before you come to Him. He'll walk with you as you determine what steps to take, resources to contact, and decisions to make.

It's through me, Lady Wisdom,
that your life deepens, and the years
of your life ripen. Live wisely and
wisdom will permeate your life.

PROVERBS 9:11–12 MSG

It's never too late to discover more about your giftedness and personality. No matter what your age or season of life, all your experiences (your family, education, jobs, talents, and disappointments) matter. They merge together to make you the unique person that you are. God wants to use your story wisely for your fulfillment and His glory. Be intentional about seeking wisdom and partner with God for a purpose-filled rest of your life.

Relationships

As iron sharpens iron,
so a friend sharpens a friend.

PROVERBS 27:17 NLT

Have you ever tried to cut a friend's hair with styling scissors that had dull blades? Or slice through a piece of steak with an unsharpened knife? It's frustrating and the results are less than satisfying. Yet when you rub the dull blade against a separate piece of iron, it works better. Likewise, when you interact with a good friend, sharing honest feedback, encouraging one another's growth, you each become wiser. How rewarding is that?

Good news from far
away is like cold water
to the thirsty.

PROVERBS 25:25 NLT

Your close friend loves you. You support and love her, too, whether she's hurting or celebrating. You can think of ways in which you're different. (She likes to eat organic food; you don't. You have four brothers; she's an only child.) But it doesn't matter. When you're apart, you miss her. You've learned how refreshing it feels to stay connected, even though it takes focused planning. And you just know God loves it when you honor your relationships.

Relaxation

She is clothed with strength
and dignity, and she laughs
without fear of the future.

PROVERBS 31:25 NLT

Take it easy! Lighten up! Chill! Mellow out!
You wish you could. But there's so much
going on. You feel the pressure. Job worries;
money, health, and family problems; that
approaching deadline—sometimes all at
once. Although you'll never be completely
stress free in this chaotic world, you can
ask God for wisdom and discernment. By
trusting Him to work in and through you,
you'll find strength to meet your daily
challenges. Then you can breathe easier
about what you face.

"First pay attention to me, and then relax. Now you can take it easy— you're in good hands."

PROVERBS 1:33 MSG

Maybe you believe you need to stay on constant alert and be just a little tense in order to prove how much you care. After all, doing God's work is serious business, right? Yet you don't have to solve all your friends' and family's dilemmas. When you try too hard to make it all just right, you lose your sense of joy. And that's no fun. God wants you to take it easy. So relax. You deserve it.

Reputation

Do not let loyalty and faithfulness
forsake you. . .so you will find favor
and good repute in the sight
of God and of people.

PROVERBS 3:3–4 NRSV

How important is a good reputation?
Some insist it must be prized at all cost.
Others say it's more crucial to develop good
character than a stellar reputation. But God
values both. According to the Bible, Jesus
increased in wisdom and favor with others
and with His Father. Although you can't
guarantee that everyone will like you all the
time, you can follow Jesus' example and live
so that you're gaining a reputation as a wise
follower of God.

*A good name is more
desirable than great riches;
to be esteemed is better
than silver or gold.*

PROVERBS 22:1 NIV

Building a godly reputation takes time.
You become known as a genuinely wise
woman by seeking God first—spending
time with Him, sharing your thoughts and
desires, reading His Word, and listening
for His Spirit's response in your heart—
Not with fanfare, but in a quiet "Here I am,
Lord" way. You become amazed by Him, and
it shows in how you treat others. Living this
way is more rewarding than being renowned
for great wealth or success.

Responsibility

A wise youth harvests
in the summer.

PROVERBS 10:5 NLT

"Y ou owe me," says someone who wants
you to finish his report and cover for him.
You're already overcommitted, but you agree
to do it. It's the story of two extremes: tired,
irresponsible person versus exhausted
woman with an exaggerated sense of
responsibility. Both of you miss the joy of a
job (and life) well done. But there's a happy
medium. It is God's wise plan that each
should be responsible for their own tasks,
mistakes, and growth. When someone's in
need, help them, but try not to shoulder the
whole burden.

A person who doesn't want to work
turns over in bed just like a door
that swings back and forth.

PROVERBS 26:14 NIRV

If you put off completing a project, you might call yourself lazy. But often procrastination is simply covert perfectionism. You believe you should do it all just right but can't (because only God is perfect), so you're disappointed in yourself. You try, stop, try again, and give up. It's like swinging in and out without making progress. The truth is, God loves you and gifted you. You can take responsibility for your own growth. You don't have to be perfect.

Rest

If you sit down,
you will not be afraid.

PROVERBS 3:24 NRSV

God loves it when you take a break from
your work and responsibilities to sit and
relax for a while. Human beings cannot
live outside their limitations. God alone
is limitless. As a wise woman, you will
recognize your human need for relief-
filled rest and respite times. Don't worry
that you'll be unproductive if you pause to
rejuvenate. Both work and rest are not only
important, but vital for healthy living.

Anyone who doesn't
want to work sleeps [her] life away.
And a person who refuses
to work goes hungry.

PROVERBS 19:15 NIRV

In case you're concerned that taking
a day off or a full-fledged vacation will
characterize you as lazy or irresponsible,
here's a tip for you: One afternoon, one
week, one month, or in some cases, one year
of respite will not an idle woman make! A
truly lazy person makes idleness a way of
life. You can, with God's help, release your
cares and worries and enjoy a little time off.

Salvation

To use a common cliché, we're all in the same boat. Every one of us needs God. Pretending you're in total control and have no spiritual need just pushes God away. Still, it may feel like you're giving up who you are and throwing yourself into the ocean without a life jacket if you release yourself and your offenses to God. Actually, the opposite is true. Coming clean before God allows Him to throw you a mercy raft.

No one can say,
"I am innocent;
I have never done anything wrong."

PROVERBS 20:9 NCV

Human beings, although created and treasured by God, are just not good enough to hit the bull's-eye of God's perfection. It's a dilemma because we long to know our Creator. The good news is we can quit working so frantically to be something that's impossible. Jesus hit the bull's-eye for us. His work on the cross makes us right with God. Ask God to show you more about what Jesus did for you.

Satisfaction

The fear of the LORD leads to life,
and [she] who has it will abide
in satisfaction.

PROVERBS 19:23 NKJV

What ties you in knots, robbing your sense of well-being? Whatever it is that keeps you feeling trapped in a cramped little box and gasping for air isn't from God. Maybe you only feel like this occasionally. Perhaps you're accustomed to it. Either way, you don't have to stay in that box. God will open the lid and release you to freedom. Give Him your life, experience His power to free your soul, and enjoy the satisfaction He longs to give.

An appetite for good
brings much satisfaction.

PROVERBS 13:25 MSG

God—and all He is and does—portrays
goodness. He is perfectly loving, kind,
forgiving, fair, patient, and good. And
although you aren't (It's a relief to admit,
isn't it?), He shares Himself with you when
you believe in His Son, Jesus. Then you grow
hungry to know Him more. He supplies your
inner longing and gives you a heart of love
for others. As you develop a healthy appetite
to do good in this world, you will experience
deep satisfaction.

Self Care

Your kindness will reward you,
but your cruelty will destroy you.

PROVERBS 11:17 NLT

What do you do when a friend shares her exhaustion or discouragement with you? Because you care, you probably listen, acknowledge her current reality, tell her how you appreciate her, remind her of recent accomplishments, or suggest she give herself a break. Today, try sharing the same responses with yourself. Harsh words rarely motivate others—yourself included. When you're kind to yourself, you flourish inside and grow into becoming the woman God designed you to be.

Above all else, guard your heart,
for everything you do flows from it.

PROVERBS 4:23 TNIV

How you feel physically affects how you think—and vice versa. Your thinking impacts your emotions which influence your actions. God chose to design you this way. Ancient scholars understood that when you protect your heart, you're actually caring for your entire being—body, mind, and soul. It's your God-given responsibility and privilege to physically, emotionally, spiritually, and mentally safeguard yourself. Wise self care honors God.

Sleep

Hold on to wisdom
and good sense.
Don't let them out of your sight. . . .
When you lie down, you won't be
afraid. . . . You will sleep in peace.

PROVERBS 3:21, 24 NCV

Keep your room cool and dark. No caffeine before bedtime. Don't watch violent TV while trying to fall asleep. Listen to calming music. Contract and relax each muscle until your body feels less tense. Take a warm bath. These are a few of the instructions experts give to those who have trouble falling asleep at night. They often work, too. Probably because they're based on good sense, research, and acquired knowledge.

Just like God's Word advised many years ago!

Follow your father's
good advice; don't wander
off from your mother's teachings.
Wrap yourself in them. . . . Wherever
you walk, they'll guide you; whenever
you rest, they'll guard you.

PROVERBS 6:20–22 MSG

What did your father and mother tell—and
show—you about working, taking care of
yourself, and managing your life? Any good
counsel you received from your parents (or
other wise mentors) is worth remembering
and heeding. God uses their past input
to give you a foundation for wise living
now. If your current sleeping and waking
routines are off-kilter, ask God to help you
implement some wise advice from your past
so you can enjoy your present life
more.

Speech

The good acquire a taste for helpful conversation; bullies push and shove their way through life. Careful words make for a careful life; careless talk may ruin everything.

PROVERBS 13:2–3 MSG

What God created for pleasure and benefit can turn against you. God created food for your nourishment, yet too much or too little causes problems. Friendships add meaning to life, but unwise relationship choices bring unnecessary pain. God blesses you with work, yet job/mission obsession often sparks burnouts. Similarly, words connect you with others, but reckless speech alienates. The good news: God doesn't leave you to wander carelessly through life. He gives you direction. Ask for what you need today.

The speech of a good person
clears the air.

PROVERBS 10:32 MSG

One way you can discover how to speak
wisely is to examine Jesus' life and
communication style. What did He say to
friends? To enemies? How did He initiate
conversation? Jesus met people in the
moment, at the point of their immediate
need. He asked them what they wanted.
He listened. Often His straightforward
responses cleared the air between
them. You can relax because you'll never
communicate perfectly like Jesus, but you
can observe His wise methods and learn.

Teachability

Whoever heeds instruction
is on the path to life.

PROVERBS 10:17 NRSV

Sometimes it's hard to take the time to heed instruction, although it would help you manage your current season more effectively. At your job, there's necessary training about new tech equipment. There's advice about health issues and information about how to better interact with friends and family. It's tempting to pretend you already know it all. Yet as a teachable woman of God, you can admit your need, accept sensible advice, and learn practical tools that will enhance your life today.

> The wise are glad to
> be instructed.
>
> PROVERBS 10:8 NLT

You make choices every day, deciding what to do and what not to do. Yet according to statistics, many make poor choices: More than one in every 100 adults in the United States is in prison. And although other countries trail America, they have many incarcerated residents, also. Countless people in this world choose to ignore instruction and face the negative repercussions. No wonder God urges you—and everyone—to seek wisdom. The wise enjoy learning and doing what's right.

Transformation

As a face is reflected in water,
so the heart reflects
the real person.

PROVERBS 27:19 NLT

Imagine sitting by a clear, cool stream
and peering at your reflection in the water.
You frown and the woman frowns back at
you. You smile and the woman smiles. You
chuckle and see the happy crinkle of your
nose. Now take a moment to look inside
your heart—at the evidence of God's love
reflected there. As a wisdom-seeking and
God-revering woman, God is in the process
of transforming your heart. Purpose today to
reflect on this hope-filled reality.

My child. . .listen
carefully to my words.
Don't lose sight of them.
Let them penetrate deep into
your heart, for they bring life
to those who find them.

PROVERBS 4:20–22 NLT

God wants to transform your heart and give you life with a capital *L*. God, the source of all wisdom, invites you to listen to all His words—words of wise advice and words about His Son, Jesus. Jesus gave His life so you can enjoy life forever with God. Don't just hear God's words and let them roll off the top of your head. Let them seep into your heart and transform you from the inside out.

Truth

Don't ever forget
kindness and truth.
Wear them like a necklace.

PROVERBS 3:3 NCV

Perhaps like many other women, you enjoy receiving and wearing gifts of jewelry. That special gold necklace instantly transforms the simple black dress you've had for years.

Living and speaking the truth with kindness and love is a little like wearing the perfect necklace. It feels, looks, and *is* lovely. Yet the truth isn't merely a nice accessory. It is an essential part of your inner life's wardrobe. Put on truth today and reflect the loveliness of God.

A truthful witness
saves lives.

PROVERBS 14:25 NIV

God loves truth telling. Wise women realize this. You'd probably never think of cheating on your taxes, fudging on your work hours, or breaking a promise to a client. But you may think it's fine to fib to yourself (or others) about a stressful, abusive, or addictive situation. Though difficult it may be, admitting the truth (the reality staring you in the face) will save lives. God wants you to tell the truth. He is on your side.

Understanding

Wisdom cries out
in the street. . .at the
busiest corner she cries out. . . .
I will make my words known to you.

PROVERBS 1:20–21, 23 NRSV

It's clear as mud." You've probably heard this expression used when describing confusion about how to deal with life, others, or God. Yet God wants to make things clear. In the midst of your busy schedule, He shares insight through the Bible and in other more surprising places. He can use any songs, books, blogs, or movies to enlighten you. You don't have to stay confused indefinitely. Ask God for discernment, remain open to learning, and expect to receive.

Wisdom is at home in
an understanding heart.

PROVERBS 14:33 MSG

Remember the day you really understood that your grandmother was your mommy's mother? A light flashed on in your little-girl head and you knew it in your heart: Grandma carried your mom in her tummy just as your mom carried you—and your little brother or sister. You saw your grandmother with a deeper level of understanding. This happens when knowledge drops from your head to your heart. It changes your misconceptions to wise truth and transforms your behavior.

Virtue

A person's insight gives
[her] patience, and [her] virtue
is to overlook an offense.

PROVERBS 19:11 HCSB

She never lets me forget it." Perhaps
you've heard a statement like this from
someone who's tired of being reminded of
a past blunder. The purpose of the frequent
reminder might be to help the offender
see her error and never do it again. But
it doesn't work. Instead it causes shame,
creates distance, and stifles reconciliation.
A virtuous woman understands that nobody
is perfect here on this earth and allows God
to take care of the rest. That's freedom.

PROVERBS 21:29 NLT

Most people think once or twice in their lifetime. The reason that I have been successful is that I think once or twice a year!" acclaimed author Victor Hugo once said. It's a humorous way of highlighting the virtue of thinking. Actually, there's an art to learning to think before you speak. Although it might be easier for an introvert and trickier for an extrovert, you should ask God to help you learn to think before you react too quickly.

Wealth

"I [Wisdom] love those
who love me, and those
who seek me find me.
With me are riches and honor,
enduring wealth and prosperity."

PROVERBS 8:17–18 NIV

Just because you look for something you've
lost doesn't necessarily mean you'll find it.
But if you genuinely seek and follow wisdom
(and God, the source of all wisdom), you
will acquire it. That in itself is a wonderful
reward. Gaining and nurturing wisdom
brings additional bonuses, too, like a
transformed attitude and persistently
courageous actions that improve your
relationships, job, and finances. You'll
experience enduring treasures—the kind
that won't get lost in a changing economy.

"For Wisdom is better than all the trappings of wealth; nothing you could wish for holds a candle to her."

PROVERBS 8:11 MSG

Wise money management makes sense. Balancing your budget, not spending more than you make, saving, making prudent investments, and prioritizing your needs and wants are all good guidelines to follow. Yet doing all these things is no guarantee that you'll be wealthy by society's standards. That's okay, because God says that nothing— even accumulating riches—can hold a candle to gaining true wisdom, knowledge, insight, and understanding. That's a legacy you can be proud to leave your children.

Words

Wise words bring many benefits.

PROVERBS 12:14 NLT

Remember, your words can set your students free and empower them." A professor repeated these words to grad students as they launched their teaching careers. Perhaps you agree with him, but if you're not a professional teacher, you wonder whether your words matter much. If you're a mother, manager, day-care worker, sister, aunt, mentor, or friend, what you say makes a significant difference. Your wise encouragement, cheerleading, concerned questions, and loving instruction will reap countless benefits for those you love.

Rash words are like sword thrusts,
but the tongue of the
wise brings healing.

PROVERBS 12:18 NRSV

Perhaps you've heard the old cliché, "Talk is cheap." This adage rings true when it refers to people who promise much yet fail to produce. But there's a flip side to this. Indeed words are not cheap. Reckless talk can start wars, producing grave consequences. And words, written in peace treaties, can stop wars. Words wield incredible power. You are privileged to offer peace-filled words of nurture, love, and kindness. Ask God to help you bring healing when you speak.

Work

Committed and persistent
work pays off.
PROVERBS 28:20 MSG

Make beds, pack lunch boxes, drive to work, answer phones and e-mails, shuttle kids, fix dinner, review homework, and start all over tomorrow. Whether you—or others—consider your work mundane or glamorous, at times it can feel boring or even insignificant. Yet satisfaction seeps into your soul when you whisper encouraging words to yourself. Try this truth-telling: *God works. Jesus worked. I work. Even creation works. Well-done work reaps God-given rewards. He values my everyday work so I will, too.*

She sets about her
work vigorously; her arms
are strong for her tasks.

PROVERBS 31:17 NIV

Although you can't do everything all at
once, you can decide daily to take care
of yourself so you'll have the necessary
strength to execute your tasks and
current roles with purpose. Even when
circumstances beyond your control make
it physically difficult to work as you'd
like, you can learn what is within your
power to do. What will help you stay strong
spiritually, mentally, and emotionally?
Remember, you are a noble and
wise woman in progress.

Worry

Worry weighs us down;
a cheerful word picks us up.

PROVERBS 12:25 MSG

Have you ever lain in bed, staring at the ceiling, recounting all that went wrong during your day? The kids acted up at church, you didn't finish your to-do list, you missed an opportunity to help a neighbor, you disagreed with your mother. . . . It all feels heavy. Try a new tactic with yourself. Instead of asking "What did I do wrong?" ask "What did I do right?" A cheerful word to yourself will lighten your load.

She doesn't worry about her family when it snows; their winter clothes are all mended and ready to wear.

PROVERBS 31:21 MSG

While trying to enjoy today, the worry bug pesters you about tomorrow, reminding you of yesterday's unpleasantness. But planning ahead stops that worry bug's incessant buzzing. Think about what you might need in order to survive your next season. Then make a plan to take care of the things you can. Of course, surprises will come, but because you've done what is in your personal power to do, you can rest and trust that you and God will face the unexpected together.

Scripture Index

Notes

Notes

Notes

Notes

Notes

Notes